WAY

How to Draw

Halloween
Things

For Jesse, Jasmine, Justin, Jordan, Melina, and Matthew

Published in the United States of America by The Child's World®
PO Box 326 • Chanhassen, MN 55317-0326
800-599-READ • www.childsworld.com

Acknowledgments
Illustration and Design: Rob Court
Production: The Creative Spark, San Juan Capistrano, CA

Registration

Library of Congress Cataloging-in-Publication Data
Court, Rob, 1956–
   How to draw Halloween things / by Rob Court.
      p. cm. — (Doodle books)
   ISBN-13: 978-1-59296-808-4 (library bound : alk. paper)
   ISBN-10: 1-59296-808-2 (library bound : alk. paper)
   1. Halloween in art—Juvenile literature. 2. Drawing—Technique—Juvenile
literature. I. Title. II. Series.

NC825.H32C68 2007
743'.893942646—dc22   2006031562

The Scribbles Institute™

Doodle BOOKS ™

How to Draw

Halloween
Things

by Rob Court

The Child's World®

jack-o'-lantern

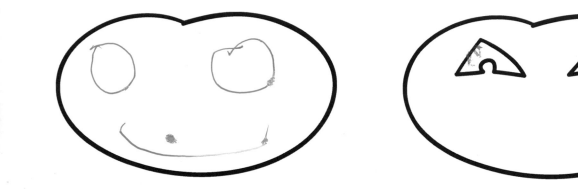

1

2

3

4

spider

1

2

4

3

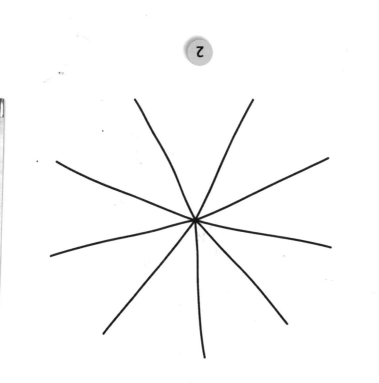

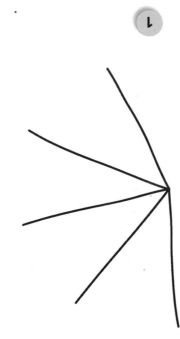

spiderweb

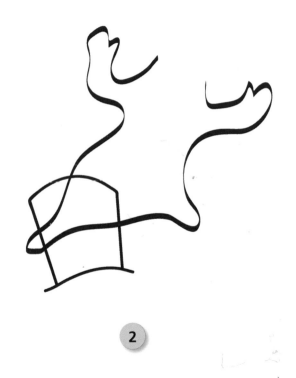

1

2

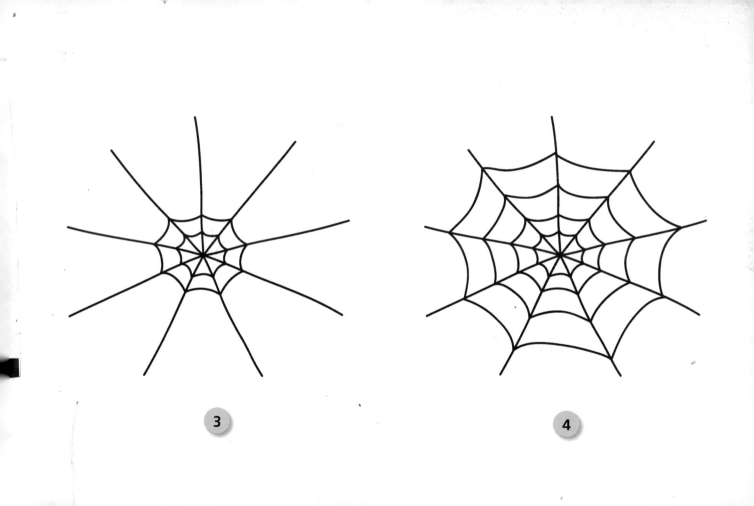

3

4

3

4

bat

1

2

3

4

skull

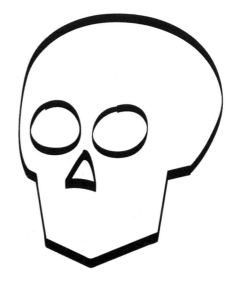

1

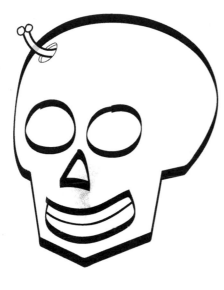

3

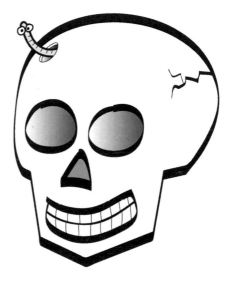

4

black cat

1

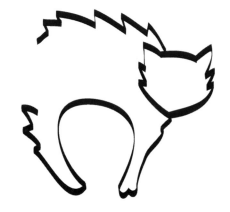

2

3

4

1

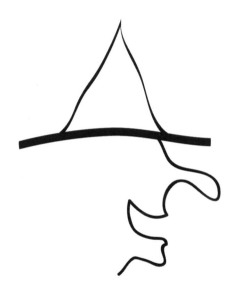

2

3

4

3

4

goblin

1

3

4

vampire

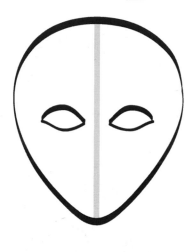

1

2

3

4

scary tree

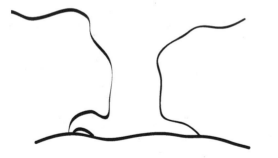

1

2

3

4

haunted house

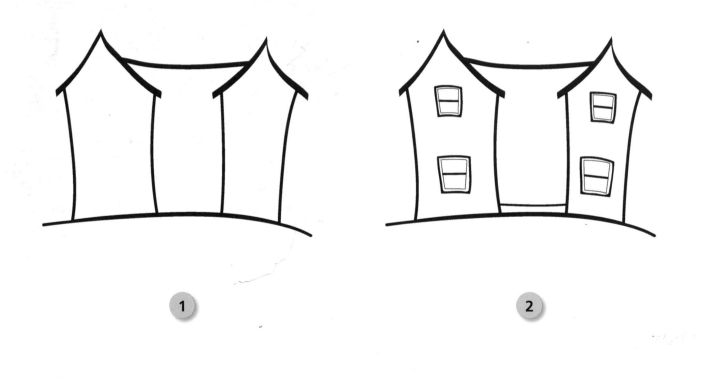

3

4

skeleton

1

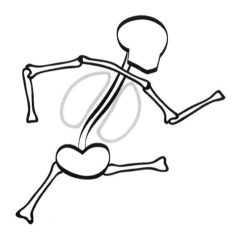

2

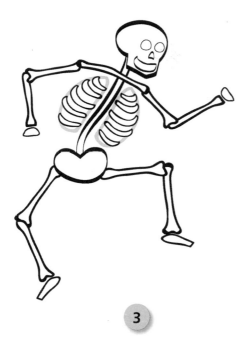

3

4

lines

horizontal

vertical

angled

curved

thick

thin

dotted

squiggly

dashed

point

Move a point to make a line.

Connect lines to make a shape.

Shapes make all kinds of wonderful things!

loop

Repeating dots, lines, and shapes makes patterns.

About the Author

Rob Court is a graphic artist and illustrator. He started the Scribbles Institute to help students, parents, and teachers learn about drawing and visual art. Please visit www.scribblesinstitute.com

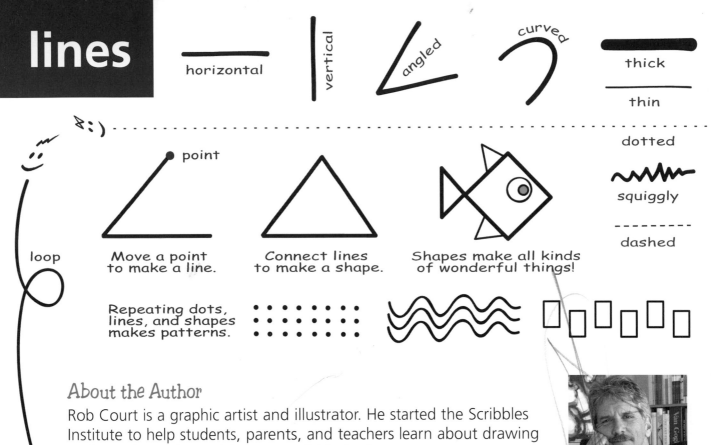